HOLLYWOODSPEAK

What they say and what they really mean!

The Official Hollywood Dictionary

By

Eugene B. Lebowitz

Publisher: W. Quay Hays
Editor: Peter Hoffman
Art Director: Kurt Wahlner
Assistant Art Director: Maritta Tapanainen

For information:
General Publishing Group, Inc.
2701 Ocean Park Boulevard, Suite 140
Santa Monica, CA 90405

Library of Congress Cataloging-in-Publication Data

Lebowitz, Eugene.
    Hollywoodspeak : the official Hollywood dictionary / by Eugene
Lebowitz.
        p. cm.
    ISBN 1-57544-001-6
    1. Motion pictures—Humor.   I. Title.
    PN1994.9.L43   1996
    818'.5402—dc20   96-22630
                                                         CIP

Printed in the USA
10 9 8 7 6 5 4 3 2 1

General Publishing Group
Los Angeles

Dedication

To my family and friends in New York
and my friends in California, who have always been
supportive. It's a shame none of them own a movie studio.

Of course
I remember you.

―――――― **MEANS** ――――――

Who the hell are you?

He always had talent.

MEANS

He's the luckiest bastard in the world.

I'm sorry, he's in a meeting.

--------- **MEANS** ---------

He's standing right here
and doesn't want to talk to you.

There was something about your script that I really liked.

—————————— MEANS ——————————

What font did you use?

Schwarzenegger and De Niro are both interested.

---- **MEANS** ----

Tom Arnold's people said they'd get back to us.

I want something totally different!

─────── **MEANS** ───────

I want *Independence Day*!

HOLLYWOODSPEAK

He's not as difficult to get along with as you've heard.

— **MEANS** —

Mother Teresa would curse him out.

Everybody here loves you!

— MEANS —

The switchboard operator
has orders not to put your calls
through.

A remake of *The Story of Louis Pasteur?* I'm perfect for the part! I've always admired the man.

--- MEANS ---

Isn't he the guy who invented milk?

HOLLYWOODSPEAK

I'm amazed at what you just told me. What a year you've had. A week after getting a film deal your father dies. Then a month later you suffer a massive heart attack. After that your house burns down, and your son is arrested crossing the border with 500 pounds of pure cocaine. It is all so unbelievable. My heart truly goes out to you.

—————————— **MEANS** ——————————

How the hell did he ever get
a film deal?!

He's got thick, straight, dark black hair. A real interesting look...who does he look like...?

—— MEANS ——

Moe or Shemp?
Shemp or Moe?

Do you have a business card?

MEANS

There's something stuck between my teeth.

I promise you!

—————————— **MEANS** ——————————

(No translation possible: means absolutely nothing.)

HOLLYWOODSPEAK

Everybody here loves you!
(def. #2)

MEANS

You're dead meat!

I wish you only the best.

——— MEANS ———

I hope you die!

No problem.

———————————— MEANS ————————————

Forget it!

No problemo.

———————— **MEANS** ————————

Youthful development person's
variation of 'forget it!'

(During warm hug)
You're the best. You made it all possible. I really couldn't have done it without you.

——————— **MEANS** ———————

This looks like a good spot to stick the knife.

I used to handle Martin & Lewis.

MEANS

I'm the one who suggested the trial separation.

I have to agree with you.

MEANS

But one day I won't have to!

HOLLYWOODSPEAK

Let me take this other call, and I'll get right back to you.

—— **MEANS** ——

Adios, sucker!

Her smile is so infectious.

--- **MEANS** ---

As are several other of her body parts.

As soon as I hang up, I'm putting you in my Rolodex.

MEANS

Right after I have your headshot tattooed on my butt!

I'll read it over the weekend.

MEANS

You'll be lucky if I get to it this year.

You have my undivided attention.

—————— MEANS ——————

Man, that new secretary's got a great ass.

No, I haven't forgotten your script. It's right on the top of my pile.

MEANS

It's the one I put my sandwich on when I'm having lunch.

Thanks for letting me take all the credit for our script. Without it I'd never be the success I am today, and I want you to know I'll never, never forget it!

—————— MEANS ——————

I owe you nothing!

It's just not right for us.

— MEANS —

My five-year-old hated it.

The most important thing in my life is my family!

---- **MEANS** ----

Man, that new secretary's got
a great ass.

Even though our numbers haven't been what we had hoped for, the network has promised to keep us on the air for another year.

—————— MEANS ——————

I got first dibs on office supplies.

It's a tough sell.

—— MEANS ——

It stinks!

I'm shocked and terribly saddened to hear about his drug problem. It's a real tragedy.

MEANS

That son of a bitch better not mention my name!

I have a film in development right now.

MEANS

Fotomat said it'd be ready this afternoon.

Thanks. I appreciate your being so honest with me.

MEANS

Asshole!

This is something we can all get behind.

——————— **MEANS** ———————

Far behind.

Just make a few small changes in the script and we'll talk.

— MEANS —

We don't like it, we'll never like it!

HOLLYWOODSPEAK

You have my word on it!

———— MEANS ————

(No translation possible: see 'I promise you!')

I think all your scripts are terrific!

—— MEANS ——

There's an empty landfill with your name on it.

**I was very touched
by what you said to me
yesterday. It's not everyday
a client pours his heart out
to me like a friend. It's all
I've been thinking about
the entire day.**

—————— **MEANS** ——————

Man, that new secretary's got
a great ass.

We'll work together again.

MEANS

Not in this lifetime!

HOLLYWOODSPEAK

Those new headshots you got are really terrific.

— MEANS —

What are you trying out for, the remake of *Bride of Frankenstein*?

Hi. Great to see you again! You look terrific.

--- **MEANS** ---

What the hell is your name?

I'm expecting my agent to call me back any minute now.

MEANS

Maybe my phone's not working?

I felt it all came together in the end.

MEANS

I fell asleep halfway through.

We've agreed to pay you scale.

MEANS

You're getting minimum!

So help me, there are no hard feelings.

MEANS

If it takes a lifetime, I'll crush you under my heel!

He fills the screen with his presence.

─── **MEANS** ───

A little of him goes a long way.

Of course I understand why you said no. It's perfectly all right.

—————— MEANS ——————

If I were God, you'd be dead!

I've been with this company longer than anyone else.

—————— MEANS ——————

Next week makes two months.

HOLLYWOODSPEAK

You're just not right for the part.

—————— **MEANS** ——————

You're too old!

I was shocked to read about him and that underage girl.

MEANS

I was expecting an underage boy.

I'll definitely read it today.

—————————— MEANS ——————————

I'll get to it when I damn well please!

I understand. It's an unbelievable opportunity, and I know you'll do great.

—— **MEANS** ——

You'll be back begging on your knees.

You want my honest opinion?

───────── **MEANS** ─────────

What lie should I tell this time?

Everybody here loves you!
(def. #3)

—— **MEANS** ——

We hate you!

HOLLYWOODSPEAK

Love ya, babe!

MEANS

You're an insignificant piece
of crap.

HOLLYWOODSPEAK

Your parties are always so interesting.

MEANS

Where else can I meet
Joe Piscopo's manager?

60

HOLLYWOODSPEAK

He's highly respected in this town.

— MEANS —

He's a butthead.

I'll read your script tonight in bed.

MEANS

Best sleeping pill in the world!

Confidentially, it's between you and one other person.

MEANS

Don't quit your day job.

I've been your biggest fan since I was a kid.

───────── **MEANS** ─────────

I thought you were dead.

If you had only called me last week.

— **MEANS** —

You still wouldn't have gotten the job.

Your script is exactly what I've been looking for.

MEANS

It's just the right size to fit under my coffee table and stop it from wobbling.

Don't worry. No one can tell you've gained any weight.

— **MEANS** —

You look like Elvis near the end.

HOLLYWOODSPEAK

I've dedicated the last half year solely to writing spec scripts.

MEANS

I haven't had a job in
six months!

I started in this business at the very bottom.

MEANS

I was there for a whole month before Dad made me vice president.

I just bought a $3 million home.

MEANS

Can you pick up lunch?

I haven't had a chance to read it—yet.

———————————— **MEANS** ————————————

My reader hasn't told me what
I think of it—yet.

You could have a real future in this business.

— **MEANS** —

With a different face, body, personality and acting ability.

Unfortunately, we are not accepting any new clients at the present time. Good luck in the future.

MEANS

Drop dead!

Nice haircut.

---- MEANS ----

I think we have a lawsuit.

HOLLYWOODSPEAK

I just don't let it get me down. It's not in my nature to be vindictive.

—————— MEANS ——————

The list is getting longer.

I had a major part in *Gandhi*.

————— **MEANS** —————

I played an Indian in the funeral procession.

HOLLYWOODSPEAK

My door is always open.

—————— MEANS ——————

Feel free to leave at any time.

It's sitting on my desk right now.

— MEANS —

Where the hell did I put that damn thing?

This part was made for you.

MEANS

And a hundred thousand
other guys.

He's a dear friend.

— MEANS —

I haven't had a chance to use
him—yet.

Everybody here loves you!
(def. #4)

—————— MEANS ——————

We really, really hate you!

You've been a wonderful audience.

MEANS

What a bunch of jerks!

With her talent I always knew she'd make it.

MEANS

She slept her way to the top.

I'm working for you.

MEANS

You're working for me.

If I didn't love this business, I wouldn't be in it!

MEANS

For half a million a year, I'd learn to love watching monkeys screw…

You were the first person I thought of!

--- **MEANS** ---

...after everyone I really wanted turned me down.

We are returning your script unread.

—————————— MEANS ——————————

We read it, we liked it, we're stealing the idea.

He'll be the next Frank Sinatra.

--------- MEANS ---------

Jr!

My client is perfect for the part.

─────────────── **MEANS** ───────────────

What is the part?

My client is perfect for the part.

MEANS

What is the part?

Run with it!

---- **MEANS** ----

As far away from here
as you can get!

HOLLYWOODSPEAK

I was wondering if you could stop by the office so we can discuss your long-term career planning.

---- MEANS ----

Start looking for a new agent.

I know talent when I see it.

MEANS

Unfortunately, you ain't got any.

I decided to take it easy for the past six months.

---- **MEANS** ----

Thank God for unemployment insurance.

**I brought your name up
at the agency, but I just
couldn't get the enthusiasm
from the others to represent
you in the way you deserve
to be represented.**

—————— MEANS ——————

You think I'd be dumb enough
to bring your name up?!

I studied improv at Second City.

MEANS

I once called out a suggestion from the audience during a show.

I'm working on
several deals.

Someone has to say yes
to one of them!

I'm in love, and this time it's the real thing.

— **MEANS** —

I got an ironclad prenuptial.

We parted because of artistic differences.

MEANS

I'm normal, he's a jerk!

I put my blood and sweat into writing this script! Tell him to take his offer and shove it!

MEANS

There are no deal breakers!

He's the hottest act in town.

MEANS

Here today, gone tomorrow.

I'm setting up a lot of meetings for you next week.

MEANS

Get off my back. No one wants to see you!

Has it been that long? It seems like only yesterday. You look wonderful.

—— MEANS ——

God, do I look that old?!

HOLLYWOODSPEAK

Tell me what you really think.

— MEANS —

I dare you.

If I were you I'd do it!

--- **MEANS** ---

If I were me I wouldn't be caught dead doing it!

Of course
I know how to
scuba dive!

MEANS

I got two days to learn how
to swim!

You only go by one name? How interesting.

--- **MEANS** ---

Look what it did for Hitler.

You haven't changed.

—————— MEANS ——————

Why not?

Win some, lose some. You can't let it make you bitter.

———— MEANS ————

I wish I had a gun!

I didn't get the part because I didn't sleep with the director!

MEANS

Why the hell didn't he ask me?!

It's not that I don't think you're talented.

MEANS

It's that no one else in this town does.

When I sign a client, it's forever!

MEANS

I'll squeeze him dry like a lemon, then toss him away.

When I sign with an agent, it's forever!

MEANS

I'll squeeze him dry like a lemon, then toss him away.

Of course I can keep a secret.

—————————— **MEANS** ——————————

And everyone I tell,
I'll tell them it's a secret.

You've still got a great pair of legs.

───── **MEANS** ─────

It's what they're holding up
that looks like shit.

We're managers.
That means we manage your career; we manage your future; we manage an overall plan to take you to the very top!

—————————— MEANS ——————————

We manage to take
50% more of your money than
an agent does.

Film is the true art form of the twentieth century.

MEANS

Pauly Shore!

I got to do what I think is right.

——— MEANS ———

I got to protect my own rear end.

We're only interested in 'high concept' ideas.

--- MEANS ---

Give us the lowest common denominator in twenty words or less.

I don't expect you to kiss the back of my feet.

MEANS

Aim a little higher.

You are a very special person. God made you, then he broke the mold.

──────── **MEANS** ────────

Or was it the other way around?

You're going to work a lot in this town.

--- MEANS ---

As a waiter!

It's definitely a go!

—————— **MEANS** ——————

Maybe, maybe not.

HOLLYWOODSPEAK

We have a commitment from Meryl Streep.

MEANS

Meryl's cousin's hairdresser
said she'd see what she
could do.

We're very close personal friends.

---- **MEANS** ----

We were just introduced.

124

There's one thing I want you to know: Trust is my middle name!

MEANS

My first name is Never!

I just signed a deal for six figures.

—————— **MEANS** ——————

So what if there's a decimal point in there!

He's decided to pursue other artistic opportunities.

MEANS

He was fired!

127

Everybody here loves you!
(def. #5)

--- **MEANS** ---

You know, we really do love you…oh, and by the way, congratulations on that three-picture deal you just signed with Spielberg.